The village of Turville on the Oxfordshire/ Buckinghamshire border, viewed from close to the Cobstone Windmill. It's a view replicated in 'Dark Autumn' (Series 4), when Barnaby walks with the flirtatious Louise August played by Celia Imrie.

LEFT AND BOTTOM
Tom Barnaby at The Lee. John, Sarah and Betty Barnaby outside The Six Bells.

BELOW
Looking past the Bull & Butcher pub to the notorious village green at Turville.

INTRODUCTION

The pilot episode of *Midsomer Murders* first appeared on ITV screens on 23 March 1997 with actor John Nettles as Detective Chief Inspector Tom Barnaby. It was a resounding and immediate success; over 13 million people watched the small-screen adaptation of Caroline Graham's novel *The Killing at Badger's Drift*. Producers Betty Willingale and Brian True-May had found a winning formula. Willingale had worked as a BBC script editor since the 1960s and was involved in some of the corporation's classic dramas: *I Claudius*, *The Barchester Chronicles*, *Tinker Taylor Soldier Spy* to name but a few. She commissioned writer Anthony Horowitz to adapt the first of the Inspector Barnaby novels and an impressive cast was assembled.

With the instant success of the pilot episode, the four remaining novels were adapted to form Series One, and appeared on screen in 1998. John Nettles, knowing that there were only five novels written for Barnaby, imagined he would soon be treading the boards back in London's West End. In all he filmed thirteen series, finally retiring from the part in 'Fit For Murder', which was broadcast in 2011.

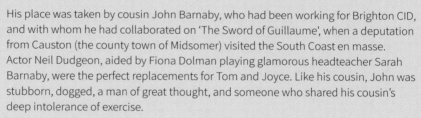

His place was taken by cousin John Barnaby, who had been working for Brighton CID, and with whom he had collaborated on 'The Sword of Guillaume', when a deputation from Causton (the county town of Midsomer) visited the South Coast en masse. Actor Neil Dudgeon, aided by Fiona Dolman playing glamorous headteacher Sarah Barnaby, were the perfect replacements for Tom and Joyce. Like his cousin, John was stubborn, dogged, a man of great thought, and someone who shared his cousin's deep intolerance of exercise.

John Barnaby has been in charge of cases from Series 14 onwards, making it an amazing total of 25 years of *Midsomer Murders* that can all be viewed via BritBox.co.uk. One of the strengths of the series, apart from the rules that Betty Willingale laid down of "no punch-ups, no car chases and as few sex scenes as possible", is the stunning English countryside in which the series is set. Episodes canter through delightful, picture-perfect villages and their inviting country pubs. This is one of the reasons why *Midsomer Murders* has been sold to so many countries around the world and can count former German Chancellor Angela Merkel as a fan. Betty Willingale described it as "Agatha Christie on speed", but it's a whodunnit with a backdrop supplied by the English Tourist Board.

This location guide takes readers on a tour of the most familiar streets, churches, pubs, village greens and cricket pitches that have appeared over the last 25 years. Armed with this guide, viewers can re-visit their favourite episodes on Britbox and play spot the village, or better still, go out and experience them for themselves. Although the full list of locations is spread across many counties, there is a tight band of familiar haunts around the Oxfordshire and Buckinghamshire border, but please be advised not to disturb the locals. As Detective Sergeant Dan Scott memorably remarks to Barnaby in 'The Maid in Splendour': "It's a typical country village, sir – full of yokels and nutters."

DCI TOM BARNABY

JOHN NETTLES

He was Betty Willingale's first choice for the part, but having devoted a decade of his life to playing Jersey detective Jim Bergerac – nine series and eighty-seven episodes – John Nettles might have been forgiven for passing up the opportunity to play DCI Tom Barnaby. What appealed to Nettles, who had spent five years working with the Royal Shakespeare Company when approached, was that Barnaby had no demons. He wasn't hooked on the bottle, stuck in a turbulent marriage, or raging against his idiotic superiors. No, he was an ordinary bloke, with a loving wife (Joyce), sensible daughter (Cully), and with no hang-ups apart from an aversion to shopping for clothes, especially with Joyce and Cully.

Against this canvas of normality could be thrown some of the most bizarre killings seen on TV in a county populated by a band of supercharged rural eccentrics who revelled in deceit, adultery and, inevitably, murder. During the Covid lockdown we saw the heat that could be generated in Parish Council meetings,

and if Jackie Weaver lived in Midsomer, it would only be a matter of days before Barnaby was parking his Volvo in the drive. Into this regular rural pageant of anger and retribution stepped the calming, unruffled figure of Tom Barnaby and the formula became a ratings winner.

Before Series Thirteen started filming John let the producers know that he wanted it to be his last. In an ITV press release, he explained: "I'd filmed over 80 episodes so I felt it was the right time to go. I didn't want to be the oldest policeman on the telly. I want to do more stage work and I see myself spending my twilight years treading the boards." Subsequently he's appeared in the BBC's *Poldark* series set in Cornwall, a perfect fit for an actor from St. Austell. He now lives near Holsworthy in North Devon and spends much of his time fighting the imposition of solar farms all around his smallholding – something that sounds like the beginning of a *Midsomer* plot.

ABOVE
DCI Barnaby directs a trio of Causton 'woodentops'.

DCI JOHN BARNABY

NEIL DUDGEON

"That one's called White Bedder; it flowers very well, right through till Autumn." These were the unlikely first lines spoken by Neil Dudgeon in *Midsomer Murders* ('Garden of Death' from Series 4) as he identified some penstemons for Joyce Barnaby in the garden of Inkpen Manor. Before he was cast as John Barnaby, Neil played randy gardener Daniel Bolt with an eye for the ladies and a sideline distilling highly alcoholic 'pumpy' in one of the outbuildings. Ten years later he would be back, but this time asking the questions and with eyes for only one lady.

Unlike cousin Tom, John Barnaby has a degree in Psychology from Durham University, something that irritates his detective sergeant Ben Jones when he first arrives in Causton. That degree not only helped his job prospects, it also introduced him to wife Sarah, who he met at university, and who plays a larger role in *Midsomer* plots than Joyce Barnaby, as Headteacher of Causton Comprehensive. Daughter Betty (named after producer Betty Willingale) came along in Series Seventeen, but it is the scene-stealing Sykes who arrived with John in Series Fourteen that really set the new Barnaby family apart from the old.

Like cousin Tom, John Barnaby likes to be the calm in the eye of the storm; the careful, slightly ponderous character who moves from suspect to suspect/guest star to guest star, assimilating the evidence as he goes. To use a cricketing analogy – and there have been a few cricketing episodes in *Midsomer Murders* – he told *Radio Times*, "I always see myself as the Geoffrey Boycott in the side, not the Flashing Blade. You get in there and you stay at the crease for

days at a time, grinding the innings out. Then you bring in Claire Bloom and she whacks the ball out of the ground. I don't really imagine people switching on *Midsomer* to watch me; I get enough of me at home."

His favourite episodes include 'A Rare Bird' (Series 14), "some great classical music"; 'The Dark Rider' (Series 15), "one of my favourite opening sequences"; 'Death of the Divas' (Series 15), "two pretty spectacular murders"; and 'The Incident at Cooper Hill' (Series 18), where locals are convinced there is a returning UFO and Barnaby himself gets arrested.

Neil Dudgeon is a big fan of the inventiveness of *Midsomer* writers: "I've always thought our deaths are sort of fantastical. They aren't the sort of ways that people are generally fretting about dying. *Midsomer*, hopefully, is a lot more fun than other series."

BELOW
Barnaby, who prefers not to be the Flashing Blade, examines a sword with DS Charlie Nelson in 'A Christmas Haunting', Nelson's first case.

DETECTIVE SERGEANTS

Where would the DCI Barnabys be without a trusted Detective Sergeant at their side; to do the considerable legwork, to be the butt of jokes and to jump to the obvious conclusion.

There have been five up until Series 22 (though Ben Jones did briefly start his nine-year shift as a Detective Constable).

DS GAVIN TROY – Daniel Casey
Series 1–7
Final Episode: 'The Green Man'
Caroline Graham wrote the part of Troy as someone a lot nastier than the role adapted by screenwriter and fellow novelist Anthony Horowitz. In the books Troy is married and a homophobe, a man with a chip on his shoulder. *Midsomer Murders'* Troy is a lot more amiable. Although Sergeant Troy wears a wedding ring in the earlier episodes, that soon disappears, allowing the on-screen Troy to have the occasional flirtation.

Daniel Casey had already played a policeman before he was cast as Troy,

having been a patrol officer in the classic BBC drama *Our Friends in the North.* When he started on the series he was 24 and so there was a much greater age difference between himself and Barnaby than there had been in the books.

Like his successor, Troy is a townie who struggles to understand country folk and is a terribly careless driver to boot. Daniel Casey set the benchmark for the Midsomer detective sergeants, including the occasional attempted dalliance with a fellow member of Causton nick. In his case it was Series 4 'Dark Autumn' where Troy gets particularly close to WPC Jay Nash, all to no avail. His final episode spent pursuing a rural tramp played by David Bradley in 'The Green Man', appeared as the first in Series 7.

DS DANIEL SCOTT – John Hopkins
Series 7–8
Final Episode: 'Midsomer Rhapsody'

Daniel Scott was next into the DS shoes, though probably larger ones as actor John Hopkins is 6´2˝ and the show's writers made much of him bumping his head all the time, on car doors, low beams in country cottages and on a church crypt light in 'The Straw Woman'. If Troy was a townie, Scott is worse, a Londoner transferred from the Metropolitan Police Force, or, as Barnaby calls them, "our friends in low places".

Scott has an initially spiky relationship with Barnaby – "don't call me Guvnor" – a lot of it stemming from his failure to understand them there locals and their country ways. He's also got one eye for the ladies. It would be difficult to imagine DS Winter spending the night with a schoolteacher persecuted by mistrustful villagers who think she's a witch. Scott doesn't take much persuading.

John Hopkins left the role in 2005 and returned to the Royal Shakespeare Company to appear with Harriet Walter (whose *Midsomer* roles have been in 'Orchis Fatalis' and 'Death of the Divas'). And he ultimately joined up with his old boss in *Poldark* in 2017, where he played Sir Francis Basset.

DS BEN JONES – Jason Hughes
Series 9–15
Final episode: 'Schooled in Murder'

By far the longest-serving detective sergeant – to both DCI Barnabys – Ben Jones is a local Midsomer lad, able to draw on his lifelong service in the local force. His slight Welsh accent can only be attributed to his parents, or his nan, who is often called on for valuable background information to cases.

When John Barnaby arrives at the start of Series 14, 'Death in the Slow Lane', there are the natural grumbles in Causton CID that maybe Jonesy should have been promoted, but just as in 'Fit For Murder' when Tom makes him SIO (Senior Investigating Officer), investigating a death at a health spa, John lets him take the lead and it's soon very clear that Ben is best at being a sergeant.

Across the 52 episodes, he was almost killed by a farm sprayer, defused a bomb by leaping across the wires, dressed up as a nun, and infiltrated a cult. His trademark expression of the puzzled double-take is beloved by *Midsomer* fans who regard him as the definitive DS. Sadly, the travelling for filming became too much for Jason Hughes, who lived

7

with his wife and daughter in Brighton. He was getting up at 4:30am to travel via London to Buckinghamshire, not getting back till 9pm in the evening and was constantly tired. In the series, he is finally promoted to Inspector… in Brighton.

DS CHARLIE NELSON – Gwilym Lee
Series 16–18
Final episode: 'Harvest of Souls'
Charlie Nelson arrives just in time for 'A Christmas Haunting' and is put up by pathologist Dr Kate Wilding, who has a spare room provided there is "no funny business". Which immediately sets the tone for their relationship as Charlie is the lodger who despairs at his landlady's messiness.

Nelson is the most athletic of the Barnaby sergeants, showing a great turn of pace in 'Let Us Prey' and 'The Dagger Club'. After Kate Wilding moves on, he challenges the next Causton pathologist, the ultra-competitive Dr Kam Karimore, to tennis matches and cycle races (you would never have got Bullard on a bike). And there's the trace of unrequited love, as Charlie is dismayed to learn that Kam has a remote boyfriend.

Gwilym Lee left after Series 18 to star in the Queen biopic *Bohemian Rhapsody* and can be seen in the C4 drama *The Great*. But who'd have known that Barnaby's assistant was the perfect fit to play rock god Brian May!

DS JAMIE WINTER – Nick Hendrix
Series 19–
First episode: 'The Village That Rose From the Dead'
Jamie Winter arrives at Causton CID soon after John Barnaby loses his greatest ever sidekick – Sykes. At the start of Series 19 Sarah Barnaby is laying a tribute to the charismatic "sprech-hund" in the garden as Winter arrives to pick up his boss. Feeling his age, Barnaby gets a bit

competitive with his new DS. Forget the death by wheel of cheese, printing press or hotwired tank, the most outrageous bit of *Midsomer* plotting comes in rugby-themed 'The Lions of Causton' when Barnaby challenges the uber-fit DS Winter to a game of squash – and wins.

When Jamie meets up with Kam Karimore, they both realise that they met on a police course five years ago and got up to a certain amount of drunken rumpus one night – and neither of them is willing to admit what happened. Just as Winter looks like making a move, Kam gets offered a job in Montreal and he's stuck with her replacement, the indomitable Fleur Perkins (Bullard in high heels and lipstick). Winter's loss is our gain.

BELOW
Gwilym Lee on the set of 'Saints and Sinners', an archaeological dig that turns nasty in Series 18.

RIGHT TOP
Barnaby and Winter investigate a sabotaged mud run in 'With Baited Breath', an episode directed by Jennie Darnell from Series 20.

RIGHT BELOW
Neil Dudgeon and Gwilym Lee bask in the reflected fame of hanging out with Sykes on Warborough Green.

SYKES
Series 13–18

Starring under his real name, Sykes the dog enjoyed a glittering career on screen before joining *Midsomer Murders* from Series 13 to 18. Prior to his spell in Causton he made appearances in *Pirates of the Caribbean* and *The Other Boleyn Girl*, and won the nation's hearts playing the role of Harvey opposite a stuffed rabbit in the ThinkBox advert (check it out on YouTube, some of his best work).

It was an impressive feat for a stray mongrel dog found wandering the streets, and handily he lived in Oxfordshire so it wasn't too far to the set. Sykes' trainer, Gill Raddings, noticed he was starting to go deaf in 2015, and so the decision was taken to retire him in 2016. He lived out his days in blissful retirement, finally going to that great boneyard in the sky in 2019.

DORCHESTER ON THAMES

OXFORDSHIRE

Once an important staging post on the road from London to Oxford with ten coaching inns, today Dorchester is a quiet backwater with only two.

Indeed it is surrounded on three sides by water, as the River Thame, which flows south-west from Aylesbury, joins the River Thames south of the town. It is the site of Dorchester Abbey, which was built by Augustinian monks on Saxon foundations from around 1170 and became a parish church after Henry VIII dissolved the monasteries. In May each year there is the Dorchester Festival – just the kind of event that the Barnabys might attend.

Dorchester Abbey with the Museum and tea rooms has made regular appearances in the series. The Museum features prominently in the episode 'House in the Woods' (Series 9) when Joyce Barnaby volunteers to help survey rural houses in peril for the local conservation society, one of which includes the eerie 'Winyard'. The area out front was used as a market in 'Night of the Stag' (Series 14). Dorchester Abbey is used in Master Class (Series 12). The

striking lychgate to the Abbey is situated right opposite the George Hotel and was seen in 'Sleeper Under the Hill' (Series 14) when vagrant woodsman Evan Jago tries to sell a stolen painting at the local market.

Historic coaching inn The George Hotel became The Feathers, employing a single mum played by Ruth Gemmell in 'The House in the Woods'. It was also at the heart of folk festival action in 'The Ballad of Midsomer County' in Series 17. Through the archway of the hotel there is a galleried yard dating to 1495, which is sometimes used in scenes. However, its greatest appearance was as The Maid in Splendour public house (Series 7) where the owner threatens to turn the 'Snug' bar into a restaurant, evicting the motley collection of locals, including 'Old Benbow', a brilliant scene-stealing performance by veteran actor Freddie Jones.

TOP LEFT
The Fleur de Lys pub, a few yards down from The George.

ABOVE
Midsomer landmark The George Hotel.

RIGHT
Dorchester Abbey and, in the foreground, the Museum.

FAR RIGHT TOP
The lychgate to Dorchester Abbey is right opposite The George.

FAR RIGHT BOTTOM
Dorchester's Post Office is no longer taking any parcels.

The White Hart Hotel on the High Street is far more upmarket than the one struggling for business in 'Small Mercies' (Series 12) run by the austere Edward Palfrey and his simpleton wife Bernice, played by Olivia Coleman. The film crew used only the exterior and switched to a Sue Ryder hostel for the interiors.

A few yards down the road from The George is the Fleur de Lys pub, which has been the Devington Arms, but featured most prominently in 'The Ballad of Midsomer County' where it was named The Captain Farrell. Melody Carver angers her uncle by playing a gig at the folk festival and wearing a certain dress.

Sadly the small post office used as Fletcher's Cross Post Office in 'Things That Go Bump in the Night' (Series 8), Morton Fendle Post Office in 'Dance With the Dead' (Series 10) and also Midsomer Newton Post Office, has closed. The stamp vending machine may have gone, but you can still post letters.

WARBOROUGH

OXFORDSHIRE

Warborough is coupled with the local hamlet of Shillingford on the River Thames, which is only a few miles downstream from Dorchester. It has all the ingredients of a *Midsomer* village: grand mansions, a colossal village green with an active cricket team, neat terraced cottages with roses entwining the doorway, plus a handsome thatched pub.

In fact, the green is one of the largest in Oxfordshire and was saved for the village – when threatened by enclosure – by the Reverend Herbert White in 1853. A plaque on the cricket pavilion is dedicated to the man '…who saved the green from Goths and Utilitarians'. The pavilion is beautifully framed in the doorway of 'The Sicilian Defence' (Series 15), where Vivian Stannington, played by Cheryl Campbell, stands in the doorway of her brother's grand house on the green.

The best introduction to Warborough on screen is at the beginning of 'Market for Murder' in Series 5 when Barnaby and Troy drive to the scene of a classic car arson and skirt the outside of the green while a cricket match is in progress. Cricket has been played on Warborough Green for near on 200 years, evidenced by

the diary of Maria Tubb, who described a game with the neighbouring village of Milton in 1831.

The pavilion was used as Badger's Drift Village Hall in 'The Great and the Good' (Series 12), and after a cricket match, players can often be seen sloping off to the Six Bells public house.

The Six Bells and The Lions at Bledlow have long been the go-to pubs for the production company, but the Six Bells is slightly ahead. It appeared in 'Bad Tidings' in Series 7, when Cully meets up with some old school friends, and in 'Left for Dead' (Series 11) under its own name. For 'Second Sight' (Series 8) it was renamed The Luck in the World, and it became The Quill Inn for 'Sins of Commission' (Series 7). For 'The Great

ABOVE LEFT
The tented village for the cycling race in 'Breaking the Chain' was set up around the old barn.

ABOVE
The Six Bells had a marquee erected on the green in front in 'The Great and the Good'.

RIGHT
Warborough and Shillingford Cricket Club pavilion.

FAR RIGHT
The terrace of private cottages opposite the pub has been used many times, both as homes and with a bit of set dressing as village shops.

and the Good' in Series 12, where a local schoolteacher is convinced she has an intruder in the house, it appeared as The Black Swan. The Six Bells has also featured in two more recent episodes which were heavily centred around the green. For 'Breaking the Chain' in Series 18 the tented village HQ of the international bike race was set up on the green, with

the pub run by Oliver (Joe McGann) and Mary (Tessa Peake-Jones). In 'With Baited Breath' (Series 21) it became The Fisherman's Arms of Solomon Gorge, where anglers hoping to catch monster fish 'The Beast' clash with fitness freaks set to take part in the Psycho Mud Run.

WALLINGFORD

OXFORDSHIRE

The historic market town of Wallingford on the River Thames is sometimes called 'the original Causton' and has many literary connections other than *Midsomer Murders*.

The Normans built a huge, strategically important castle at Wallingford and it remained an important Royalist stronghold until after the English Civil War, when the victorious Oliver Cromwell had it demolished. On a less historical note, in *Three Men in a Boat* Jerome K. Jerome recounts the story of a riverside inn at Wallingford where a succession of locals drop by and claim *they* caught the handsome stuffed trout in a cabinet. Then George climbs up to get a better view and accidentally pulls it off the wall, only to find the fish was made of plaster. The other literary connection is that queen of the whodunnit Agatha Christie lived in the town from 1934 until her death in 1976. Visitors can follow an Agatha Christie trail around the town.

Wallingford Corn Exchange in the Market Square is the most recognisable *Midsomer* building and appeared as Causton Playhouse in many early episodes, such as 'Death of a Hollow Man' in Series 1, when a production of *Amadeus* goes horribly wrong, 'Death's Shadow' (Series 2) and 'Death of a Stranger' (Series 3). In this episode Cully is busy learning her lines for a production of *The Importance of Being Earnest,* and the opening night at the Playhouse provides a vital clue for Barnaby when he sees a photo from the 1970 production.

More recently, the market square and town were used as the finish for a cycle race in Series 18, 'Breaking the Chain', where Charlie Nelson and Kam Karimore fail to have any fun on their fun ride.

BELOW
Wallingford Corn Exchange.

BOTTOM
Wallingford Market Square.

BELOW LEFT
A boathouse on the Thames near Wallingford. In 'The Sting of Death' DS Winter investigates a narrowboat moored alongside.

MAPLEDURHAM

BERKSHIRE

The estate of Mapledurham stretches back to Norman times, but the grand house used in *Midsomer Murders* was built in the late 16th and early 17th centuries.

Sir Michael Blount was a high official in the court of Elizabeth I and in 1588 borrowed £1,500 to create a home befitting his status. The house was besieged and sacked by Parliamentarians in 1643 and his grandson Sir Charles Blount, who had inherited the house, was killed during the Siege of Oxford.

Fast forward to 2010 when it was used in 'Dark Secrets' as a stately pile lived in by elderly recluses William and Mary Bingham, played by Edward Fox and Phyllida Law. The cranky couple appear to live on frozen pizzas and the *Daily Telegraph*, stacks of which are piled up around the house.

The ancient water mill at Mapledurham, which made a memorable appearance in the film *The Eagle Has Landed*, was used extensively in the Series 7 episode 'The Fisher King', where it was the home of Nathan Green played by Jim Carter.

Keen observers might have noticed an Exit sign in the hallway of Bingham House. Mapledurham is still in private hands, but tours are offered. From 2022, visitors will be able to opt for two different tours; one featuring the house, the other the watermill, turbine, and St. Margaret's Church next door.

TURVILLE

OXFORDSHIRE

Midsomer Parva or Dibley? Geraldine Granger had a much happier ending to her time in the village of Turville than the vicar in *Midsomer Murders*' 'Straw Woman'…

Halfway between Henley and High Wycombe, the village of Turville is one of the most filmed locations in England. For a start, high above the cottages and the flintstone walls is the Cobstone Windmill, the cinematic home of Caractacus Potts and his family in *Chitty Chitty Bang Bang*. The village itself was home to the *Vicar of Dibley* and it featured prominently in *Goodnight Mister Tom* and in the first series of *Killing Eve*. *Midsomer Murders* staged one of their most spectacular episodes here as a nod to 70s cult classic *The Wicker Man*.

Like Haddenham, Turville can trace its history to the Dark Ages and is listed in the *Anglo-Saxon Chronicle* of 796 as Thyrefield. The church of St. Mary the Virgin has its origins in the tenth century and is at the heart of the small village. In front is a large wooden bench carved

from the trunk of a tree which can be glimpsed in many episodes. Beyond that is an innocuous-looking triangle of grass. To call it a village green might be stretching the description, but it is on this spot that one of the most barbarous murders in *Midsomer* history was committed. In the 'Straw Woman' (Series 7), the village curate was drugged and placed in a ceremonial bonfire that was lit by an unsuspecting vicar. And that's just the start of the fun, with mysterious cases of spontaneous combustion causing villagers to claim that the progressive local teacher is a witch. For this episode, the popular local pub, the Bull & Butcher, appeared as The Oak – built on the site of the oak tree where the village traditionally hanged its witches – and it also made an appearance in 'Murder on St. Malley's Day' (Series 5) as the Chalk and Gown

public house, when pupils from a posh local boarding school hire a private room for a party. For the infamous death-by-wheel-of-cheese episode, 'Schooled in Murder' (Series 15), the pub was renamed The Spotted Cow, while in 'Death by Persuasion' (Series 19) it received a literary renaming. The episode about murderous deeds at an immersive Jane Austen weekend has Barnaby and Winter dressing up in Regency clobber and the Bull became The Captain Wentworth, the heroic sea captain in *Persuasion*.

FAR LEFT
A church where Geraldine Granger would definitely feel at home.

LEFT
The Bull & Butcher public house has its own commemorative *Midsomer* plaque.

BELOW LEFT
A view looking down on Turville from the footpath leading up to the Cobstone Windmill.

BELOW
Boys from Devington School sprint through this scene during the St. Malley's Day Race.

HAMBLEDEN AND FINGEST

BUCKINGHAMSHIRE

Hambleden and Fingest are two neighbouring villages between Henley and High Wycombe, and a stiff walk from the village of Turville; indeed, when driving between Hambleden and Fingest you can see Turville's Cobstone Windmill high on the hill.

ABOVE
Hambleden's village shop was seen in 'Blood Will Out'.

Recorded in the Domesday Book of 1086 as Hambledene, the well-preserved village with its flintstone walls has many Grade II-listed cottages. In 1944 it hosted US troops prior to D-Day, so it was fitting that *Band of Brothers*, the WWII series based on Major Dick Winters' war record, should be filmed here. St. Mary's Church, which dates from the 12th century, was used in 'Blood Will Out' in Series 2 when Troy is made to climb the church tower and observe the slippery Orville Tudway in his Romany caravan through binoculars.

The lychgate and war memorial are also much in evidence in Series 16, 'Wild Harvest', during a farmers' market held in the village of Midsomer Wyvern. It's an episode that revolves around top restaurant Wyvern House and its rude and critical Scottish chef Ruth Cameron, who is married to the ex of local pub landlady Angela Linklater.

The pub in question is The Stag & Huntsman, one of the many *Midsomer* old favourites. It has appeared in 'Who Killed Cock Robin?' (Series 4), 'Down Among the Dead Men' (Series 9) and in

'The Glitch' (Series 12), an episode starring David Haig as keen cyclist and history buff George Jeffers. Many parts of the village can be seen in 'The Glitch', but the ancient Aspen Arms, outside which DS Jones and Barnaby have lunch while discussing the case, is actually The Royal Standard of England in Forty Green (see page 44).

Not far from Hambleden and still within the parish boundary is Fingest, home of The Chequers Inn and the village where astrologer 'Mystic Mags', played by Maureen Lipman, lived in 'Written in the Stars' (Series 15). The Chequers has featured in 'Country Matters' (Series 9), 'The Silent Land' (Series 13) and 'A Dying Art' (Series 18), but its most recent appearance was in the Series 21 episode unofficially dubbed 'Strictly Come Midsomer Dancing' and officially titled 'The Point of Balance', all about a ballroom dancing contest. Anguished computer programmer Warren Cunningham makes a confession to Barnaby and Winter in the pub garden, but things are not all they seem…

TOP LEFT
The Stag & Huntsman pub on the street where the final denouement of 'Wild Harvest' is played out.

LEFT
St. Mary's Church and lychgate in Hambleden.

TOP RIGHT
The church of St. Bartholomew's at Fingest, seen from Mystic Mags' garden in 'Written in the Stars'.

ABOVE LEFT
The Chequers Inn at Fingest.

BLEDLOW
BUCKINGHAMSHIRE

With a beautiful Chiltern Hills backdrop, Bledlow is a perfect Midsomer location. Both Barnaby couples have used the church, but for entirely different purposes…

Bledlow sits on the Buckinghamshire side of the Oxfordshire border, just a stone's throw from the ancient Roman road, the Icknield Way. There has been a settlement at Bledlow since Anglo-Saxon times, and although it has its own cricket club, it is more of a hamlet than a village. However, it does have those essential ingredients of an English village – a pub and a church. And it is to these two institutions that *Midsomer Murders* has returned time and again.

Holy Trinity Church at Church End became Badger's Drift Church in the very

first episode shot in 1996 and aired in 1997. Tom Barnaby was back in Series 2, when he and Joyce decide to renew their wedding vows on their 25th wedding anniversary, meeting up with the scheming vicar of St. Michael's, played by Richard Briers.

Throughout Midsomer, local pubs have the unfortunate tendency to hire publicans that stray onto the wrong side of the law, while the church does a strong line in devious vicars. In Series 16 the church became St. Cicely's, at the heart of Midsomer Cicely, where the choir

ABOVE
The Lions at Bledlow is one of *Midsomer Murders* most visited pubs.

BELOW
Holy Trinity Church at Bledlow was used as St. Cicely's.

progress out of the church at ten past six on St. Cicely's day morning. Although observant locals might notice that for one day of the year the sun appears to be rising over Bledlow in the West not the East. In the same episode 'Saints and Sinners' a murder is committed in the graveyard just yards away from where elderly orchid expert Emily Simpson was buried in the pilot programme. Bringing us right up to date, in a recent episode, 'The Sting of Death' (Series 21), John and Sarah Barnaby attend a pop-up yoga class held in the church, much to the annoyance of the reverend Nigel Brookthorpe, played by Derek Griffiths, who threatens some very unholy retribution.

Only a stroll down the road is the quintessential *Midsomer Murders* public house, The Lions at Bledlow. Formed from three cottages knocked into one building, it has its roots in the 16th century and is the typical low-beamed English pub with inglenook fireplaces, horse brasses and traditional beer pumps. When the Barnaby family go house hunting in Series 2, 'Dead Man's Eleven' they sit outside of what appears to be the Queens Arms, while in 'King's Crystal' it has transformed itself into

The Dog & Partridge. We get a good look at the triangular green outside at the opening to 'Birds of a Feather' (Series 14), when jack-the-lad handyman Dave Foxley, played by Paul Nicholls, drives his pick-up past The Feathers public house. It also made an appearance in 'Blue Herrings', and in 'Dark Autumn' Barnaby takes part in the pub's hotly contested Aunt Sally competition. One of its greatest roles was in Series 19 as The Hope & Anchor, in the tale of cricketing skulduggery 'Last Man Out', where it was at the heart of a match-fixing scandal.

RIGHT
Archaeologist Alex Dyer is lured to this spot in 'Saints and Sinners'.

BELOW RIGHT
View through the church gate to Emily Simpson's Beehive Cottage.

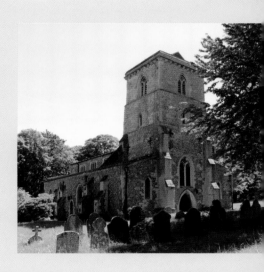

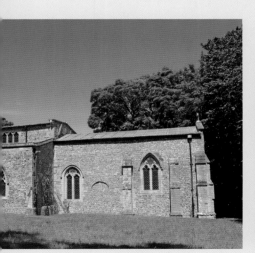

SYDENHAM

OXFORDSHIRE

The small village of Sydenham was at the heart of the action in the folk festival episode, 'Ballad of Midsomer County', with an American legend behind the bar of the local pub.

Sydenham is the other side of the Icknield Way from Bledlow, across the county line in Oxfordshire and about 3 miles from Thame. The Manor of Sydenham was established in Saxon times, but after the Norman conquest, 'Guillaume le Vanquer' gave it to one of his closest advisors, William FitzOsbern. FitzOsbern died in 1071 and, after his perfidious son Roger de Breteuil took part in the failed 'Revolt of the Earls' against William in 1075, the king took it back.

The distinctive church in the village is St. Mary's, with parts dating back to the Norman period. It is one of the few in South Oxfordshire with a wooden tower, which was restored in the Victorian period. In *Midsomer Murders* it appeared in 'Night of the Stag' (Series 14) when the Reverend Walker clashes with the grotesque local publican, played by Warren Clarke, who wants the villagers of Midsomer Abbas* to re-enact an ancient rural fertility tradition. *The 'Abbas' is

TOP
Parts of St. Mary's Church date back to the 13th century.

ABOVE
Sydenham bus stop and open-air library.

presumably a nod to the Cerne Abbas Giant chalk hillside carving of an ancient man carrying a large club.

Opposite the church is the The Crown public house that was adorned with hunting trophies and renamed The Stag for the villagers' rampaging stag night. It's clearly a useful space to film in, because it provided the interior for The Green Man in 'Murder by Magic' and also the interior of the Captain Farrell in 'The Ballad of Midsomer County' (Series 17). Fans of the gritty urban cop drama *The Wire*, shot on the drug corners of Baltimore, would no doubt have been amazed to see detective Lester Freamon, actor Clarke Peters, sat in a pub in rural Oxfordshire playing a pub landlord.

Other places around the village were used for the Folk Festival, including the former junior and infants school dating from 1849. The last child left in 1948, and since then it's been the Village Hall. In 'Night of the Stag' it was used as a temporary Incident Room by Barnaby and Jones, while in 'The Ballad of Midsomer County' it becomes the office of festival organiser Brian Grey who, late one night, makes the fatal *Midsomer* mistake of going to investigate a strange noise armed with only a "hello…?" One feature of the real-life village shows the sense of community in Sydenham. Next door to the red telephone box that has been turned into a heart defibrillator, is the old bus stop. There may be few buses passing now, so instead it has been turned into a mini open-air library.

THAME

OXFORDSHIRE

The town of Thame has seen its fair share of bloodshed over the years. During the Civil War in the 1640s the town was occupied in turn by Royalists and by Parliamentarians. After the Battle of Chalgrove Field in 1643, one of the leading Parliamentarians, Colonel John Hampden, who had been educated at Thame Grammar School, died of his wounds here.

There are several exhibits that commemorate the English Civil War in Thame Museum at 79 High Street. It's where DS Jones drops in to check on an apparently motiveless burglary in 'Secrets and Spies' (Series 11) and gets propositioned by saucy curator Amanda Watson, who's clearly very well acquainted with "Jonesy".

In the early series of *Midsomer Murders*, the production crew were regular visitors to Thame. Dominating the High Street is the Grade II-listed Thame Town Hall

(1887), which was used as Causton Arts Centre for 'The Maid in Splendour', when Dan Scott and Cully go to see a film society screening of *The Seventh Seal* directed by Ingmar Bergman – and Cully accuses Scott of going to sleep. In Series 11, 'Shot at Dawn' it appears as Causton Town Hall, with Barnaby and Jones dashing out in the rain discussing a World War 1 re-enactment by the Royal Midsomer Yeomanry.

One of the famous residents of Thame, apart from former Bee Gee Robin Gibb,

ABOVE
The unmistakeable Thame Town Hall.

BELOW
The Black Horse, very close to the offices of *Midsomer Life* magazine.

was the great Irish poet W. B. Yeats, who lived at 42 Lower High Street in 1921, right next to the impressive Six Bells pub. This is one of many inviting pubs in Thame that Barnaby hasn't visited on official business, including the precarious half-timbered Birdcage pub, which dates back to the 14th century, with many historic residents supposedly still reappearing. Like the Town Hall, it's built on the Middle Row, the line of buildings which occupies the centre of what was once a prodigiously wide medieval High Street.

A little further up the street is the Spread Eagle Hotel, renamed as The Morecroft Hotel in 'Midsomer Life'– a Series 11 episode about a glossy county magazine, with an office in the centre of Thame. It's where Barnaby has to intervene in a fight in the bar between locals and some cockney off-roaders 'dahn from London' to get their vehicles muddy. A little further on is The Black Horse, the pub where John Barnaby drops in during his first Causton investigation during 'Death in the Slow Lane' (Series 14).

BELOW LEFT
The Swan Hotel appears in 'Vixen's Run' (Series 9).

BELOW
The Spread Eagle Hotel.

BOTTOM
Thame Museum, the interiors of which were used as Causton Museum where curator Amanda makes an exhibition of herself in 'Secrets and Spies'.

LONG CRENDON
OXFORDSHIRE

Long Crendon is a small village north-west of Thame, about 3 miles from Haddenham, that has appeared in many episodes over the years.

The village has nearly 100 cottages listed by English Heritage and two manor houses, though it's the manor on Frogmore Lane that has played the many starring roles. The other manorial house, the former Abbots House from Notley Abbey, was owned by Laurence Olivier and Vivienne Leigh between 1948 and 1954. So the village has a history of entertaining actors.

Starting at one end of the old High Street, The Courthouse next to St. Mary's Church dates from about 1485, where it held meetings of the manorial court on the upper floor. It was the second property to be acquired by the fledgling National Trust in 1900 and can still be visited

today. It was used as the bookshop run by Bella Summersbee at the centre of the Luxton Deeping Crime Festival in 'The Dagger Club' in Series 17.

Before you get to the Eight Bells pub, the thatched cottage known as Madges (not open to the public) was dressed up with signage to transform it into The Belleville Inn, the country hotel that allowed pets to roam at will in 'Red in Tooth & Claw' (Series 19). The half-timbered building to the left of the arch was formerly a barn.

Early episodes of *Midsomer Murders* showed the Eight Bells pub with its old pub sign. It has appeared as the Florey Arms of Ford Florey in 'Blood on

the Saddle' (Series 13), 'A Tale of Two Hamlets', where the set designers carefully placed rubbish all over the village, and in Series 14, 'The Oblong Murders', where John Barnaby quizzes the publican about two former regulars who died in a boating explosion. And Jonesy gets pelted with tomatoes. A decade earlier, Neil Dudgeon was seen as Daniel Bolt storming off up the road with the pub in the background after a heated village meeting in 'Garden of Death' (Series 4).

That meeting was held in Long Crendon's village hall, Church House, which became the village shop in 'Tainted Fruit' and a library in Blood Wedding (Series 11). It's also the place where the local youth gather outside to challenge Danny Merrick to visit 'The House in the Woods'.

Opposite Church House is an often-used private residence, Well Cottage, which featured in 'Blood on the Saddle' in a memorable Western-style opening sequence when a gun-toting stranger

rides into the village of Ford Florey and kicks open the door.

To the end of the High Street and across the Bicester Road there is the familiar-looking Frogmore Lane and the arched entrance to Long Crendon Manor. It has been the star of many episodes, particularly 'The Axeman Cometh', about a 60s rock band reuniting, where one of the cast emulates the tragic death of Rolling Stone Brian Jones and ends up in the swimming pool. It was also the setting for the memorable 'A Christmas Haunting' in Series 16, the first case for DS Charlie Nelson, where a ghost-hunting party in Morton Shallows turns murderous one frosty night. Earlier still it was Inkpen Manor, where the heartless owner wanted to dig up the memorial garden and turn it into a tea room for visitors, causing untold distress in the village. Today, Long Crendon Manor hosts weddings, and you can book an overnight stay in the grand house that dates back to 1660.

OPPOSITE TOP
Long Crendon Manor, Gary Cooper's gaff Badgers Hall in 'The Axeman Cometh'.

LEFT
The Eight Bells public house.

TOP LEFT
The Courthouse and St. Mary's Church.

ABOVE
Madges cottage.

ABOVE LEFT
Well Cottage.

HADDENHAM

BUCKINGHAMSHIRE

There are two significant village ponds in *Midsomer Murders* – Aldbury in Hertfordshire has one, but the most frequently seen is at Church End in Haddenham

Queen Elizabeth I once owned the village of Haddenham, which can trace its roots back to Anglo-Saxon times. It's a regular location for *Midsomer Murders* and the home of St. Tiggywinkles, the charity caring for injured wild animals, in particular hedgehogs. Haddenham is a village with distinctly old and new parts; the picturesque duck pond at Church End being the old, with a more modern part near the railway station. There's a strong sense of community in the village, exemplified by the fabulous Scarecrow Festival in July.

The village has had many guises. It was Little Kirkbridge in 'Judgement Day', one of the contenders in a best-kept village competition where Joyce Barnaby was subjected to repeated Morris dancing, while in 'Crime and Punishment' (Series 16) it became the lawless Bleakridge, where residents were so fed up with the incidence of crime that they band together and form their own neighbourhood patrol, the Bleakridge Watch. Other episodes include 'A Talent for Life', 'Orchis Fatalis', 'Vixen's Run', 'Maid in Splendour' and 'Midsomer Life'.

Nearby Aylesbury is famous for its ducks, and the duckpond in front of the Norman church of St. Mary's was once used to breed them. The church is featured

RIGHT AND BELOW RIGHT
Two views of Church End's historic duck pond. Once there were four.

BELOW
St. Mary's Church. The route to the village primary school passes through the churchyard.

BOTTOM LEFT
The Green Dragon pub.

BOTTOM RIGHT
A magnificent Gruffalo scarecrow from Haddenham's Scarecrow Festival. Long Crendon has one, too.

in 'Birds of Prey' (Series 6) and made a starring performance as St. Cyprian's in 'Murder by Magic' in Series 17, where the vicar grants permission for a spectacular illusionist performance in the church that goes horribly wrong, much to the disgust of the curate Andrew Maplin, who cannot stand such an abomination in the house of god. Next door to the church is Margaret Winstanley's cottage from 'Orchis Fatalis', which was then turned into a community café run by Barbara Walton and her retired GP husband Duncan in 'Crime and Punishment'. Although in Duncan's case, punishment is actually pleasure…

DCI John Barnaby visits The Green Man public house in 'Murder by Magic'. In real life it was the Green Dragon gastropub; however, in May 2021, against the wishes of Buckinghamshire Council, a change of use was granted for it to become a private residence. This followed the closure of the Rose and Thistle pub less than 200 yards away. In 'Crime and Punishment' it became The Gallows, a struggling pub run by Mitch McAllister (Neil Morrissey) and his partner Lena.

CUDDINGTON
BUCKINGHAMSHIRE

Like many of the *Midsomer* villages, Cuddington is in Buckinghamshire near the Oxfordshire border. It dates from Anglo-Saxon times, when it was 'Cudda's estate', and today its main claim to fame is winning best-kept village competitions.

*M*idsomer Murders haven't used the chocolate-box-perfect thatched cottages on the Aylesbury Road in Cuddington, but they *have* used the village shop. Unlike many rural outposts, Cuddington has managed to retain its Post Office, and the shop was used in Series 3, 'Death of a Stranger', when a tramp comes in to buy cider, and later as a specialist paranormal shop, in 'Talking to the Dead' (Series 11).

The village hall, Bernard Hall, was built in medieval style in 1933 by Colonel Francis Tyringham Bernard, who gave it to the village. It has recently been upgraded with the latest digital projector technology so that first-run films can be shown in High Definition as part of the Village Picture House project. The hall was used as an incident room in 'Death of a Stranger' and

as the venue for the unforgettable Spanish Evening at the start of 'Bad Tidings' in Series 7. It can also be seen in 'Death and Dreams' in Series 6, where the village band – winners of the Morton Fendle Concert Championship, no less – return for practice, after a quick tuneless march down Long Crendon High Street.

Next door is a thriving primary school, and right opposite that is the church of St. Nicholas. Barnaby visits the church when he goes to see the WWI graves of Douglas Hammond and Thomas Hicks, military veterans (played by Sir Donald Sinden and George Cole) representing the two feuding families in 'Shot at Dawn'. With a handsome pub – The Crown on the Aylesbury Road – Cuddington has all the ingredients of a well-preserved rural village adapting to the 21st century.

TOP LEFT
Cuddington Post Office continues to serve the village.

ABOVE
The Bernard Hall, scene of much flamenco in Series 7.

LEFT
St. Nicholas Church; the graveyard was used in Series 11.

BELOW AND BOTTOM
The Crown Public House on the Aylesbury Road and one of the beautifully maintained thatched cottages that has helped Cuddington pick up multiple best-kept village awards.

WORMSLEY PARK

BUCKINGHAMSHIRE

This beautiful, quintessentially English cricket ground in the heart of the Chiltern countryside was built by the American-born philanthropist Sir Paul Getty. Getty was the elder son from the fourth marriage of John Paul Getty and inherited much of his father's fortune. Some time in the 1970s he was introduced to cricket by one of his neighbours, Sir Mick Jagger. Getty gradually fell in love with the game and what he perceived as its traditional British values. The distinctive thatched pavilion was opened in 1992 and the ground hosts celebrity matches and Minor Counties games involving Buckinghamshire. It featured prominently in Series 12, 'Secrets and Spies', but was centre stage for much of 'Last Man Out' in Series 19, when Ben Jones returns to Causton on an undercover mission to root out match fixing in a new one-day cricket league, which some members of Lower Pampling Cricket Club cannot abide.

BELOW
A more conventional match at the Sir Paul Getty ground, which has a traditional red telephone box behind the pavilion.

BRILL
BUCKINGHAMSHIRE

Brill is about 4 miles north-west of Long Crendon and known for its windmill, which has timbers that date to 1865. It is one of the earliest examples of a post mill and is Grade II listed. Ownership passed to Buckinghamshire County Council just after World War II, but the necessity of installing a supportive steel structure in 1967 meant that the windmill could no longer turn to face the wind. Local conservation groups have helped restore the woodwork over the years and it is a popular destination for walkers.

The windmill is open to the public on various days of the year and has featured in more than one episode of *Midsomer Murders*. In 'A Tale of Two Hamlets' (Series 6) written by Alan Plater, it was at the heart of the action as the home of Sarah Proudie in an episode about two warring villages. Most recently it was the home of painter Eric Gladberry in 'The Wolf Hunter of Little Worthy' (Series 22). Barnaby goes to visit him to ask about his son Jez, and finds that he stubbornly refuses to include the glamping site in his paintings.

ABOVE
The windmill at Brill is easily accessible.

THE LEE
BUCKINGHAMSHIRE

It was the original Badger's Drift and soon became the village of Marshwood, with the village green playing host to several meetings of the Marshwood Hunt

The village of The Lee near Great Missenden is far removed from central London, but there is a strong connection. The village was once owned by the Liberty family, proprietors of the famous half-timbered Liberty furniture and design store on Regent Street. They used timbers from the former 121-gun ship-of-the-line HMS *Howe* for the premises and also for their house in the village. The grand figurehead of Lord Howe that adorned the ship – designated an ancient monument – still resides in The Lee but is now too fragile to move.

Midsomer Murders fans will recognise the village immediately, as it appeared in the very first programme as Badger's Drift, and in one of the most recent episodes 'The Stitcher Society' (Series 22), where many of the villagers belong to an exclusive club supporting survivors of open-heart surgery. One of the members, outrageous estate agent Mimi Dagmar (a bravura performance by Hannah Waddington), even tries to seduce DCI Barnaby. In between, the village has appeared in 'Death of a Hollow Man'

(Series 1), 'Death's Shadow' (Series 2), 'Death of a Stranger'(Series 3), which starts with the local fox hunt meeting on the village green, and 'Painted in Blood' (Series 6).

One of the distinguishing features of the green is the circular seat beneath the oak tree in the centre of the green. In earlier episodes it is wooden, but more recently it has been replaced by a painted metal seat with enough tree clearance for future growth. This is often the place for earnest discussions between characters, such as step-brother and step-sister Timothy Argo and Stella Starling in 'Drawing Dead' (Series 20), when it was wooden, but by the time Toby Wagner is threatened by dogs in 'Stitcher Society' it was metal.

At one end of the green is the War Memorial that is often prominent, such as when Isaac Starling, who is campaigning to be village sheriff in 'Drawing Dead', berates Barnaby and Winter for doing a poor job and shows them some video of his own.

The monument, in the form of a Celtic cross, was dedicated in 1921 to villagers who lost their lives in the Great War, including six pairs of brothers. Nine local men died at the Battle of Fromelles in 1916, which must have had a tremendous impact on the village.

The Cock & Rabbit pub, also at the bottom end of the green, is a popular location too. It had a major role in 'Stitcher Society' and was also involved in 'Saints and Sinners' (Series 18), where it posed as The Rose and Chalice of Midsomer Cicely, hosting archaeologists digging up the bones of what they believed was the real St. Cicely. It can also be seen in 'Death of a Stranger' and 'Death in a Chocolate Box'. At the time of writing, it was up for sale.

CHENIES MANOR

BUCKINGHAMSHIRE

Chenies Manor House is a building with architectural secrets. It was once known as Chenies Palace, with a much bigger range of buildings that hosted Henry VIII and his considerable retinue.

Chenies Manor House is a Grade I-listed Tudor building once occupied by the Cheney family, which passed to John Russell, 1st Earl of Bedford, in 1526. Like the ill-fated Cardinal Wolsey, Russell was a prominent advisor to Henry VIII, and while Wolsey built Hampton Court only for Henry to take an irresistible shine to it, Russell managed to hang on to the palace that he constructed. With precious little documentation of the house and

demesne that stood in the 16th century, architectural historians have struggled to put together an accurate picture of the house which Henry visited, but scientific dating of beams and roof timbers date much of the house to around 1550. The manor, with various additions and subtractions, remained in the possession of the Russell family until it was sold in 1954. Today, it is owned by the Macleod Matthews family, who have created

ABOVE LEFT
The main entrance at Chenies Manor.

ABOVE RIGHT
Two views of the distinctive Chenies garden with its elaborate summer house.

LEFT
Tamara Deddington (Imogen Stubbs) shows Barnaby and Winter around the bee-friendly garden at Apley Court in 'The Sting of Death'.

beautiful gardens and opened up a large part of their home – with its medieval well, dungeon and priest hole – for garden visits, afternoon tea, and guided tours of the house. You can get married here, too, as the parish church of St. Michael is right next door.

It is a regular haunt of *Midsomer Murders* (as well as John Russell, whose tomb is in the church), and first featured in 2000 in the episode 'Judgement Day' as the home of retired actor Edward Allardice, played by Moray Watson in a cast that included Hannah Gordon, Timothy West and two teenage village chancers played by Orlando Bloom and Tobias Menzies. Whatever happened to them…?

An episode later it was back as the Aspern Hall Museum, where paintings get mysteriously slashed in 'Beyond the Grave', an episode starring Prunella

Scales. Quite fittingly, for a property that contains its own physic garden, it became Malham Manor, host of the Midsomer Malham Flower and Orchid Show in 'Orchis Fatalis' in Series 8.

Series 14 saw the manor used as the headquarters of The Oblong Foundation, a controlling cult which DS Jones infiltrates in 'The Oblong Murders'. It was then home to 'maestro' Michael Falconer, the temperamental musical genius who was keen to debut his ninth symphony at the Thassingham Music Festival in Series 19, 'Curse of the Ninth'.

Finally, the white birdcage summer house was much in evidence in Series 21, 'The Sting of Death', when the garden was populated with beehives belonging to Ambrose Deddington, tending his unique Apley Court bees and harvesting their regenerative honey.

HURLEY
BERKSHIRE

Hurley, on the River Thames, is a few miles east of Henley and close to the starting point of Henley Regatta rowing races. The river has featured in quite a few episodes, along with the nearby Hambleden Lock.

The Thames played a significant part in 'Let Us Prey', where a macabre medieval fresco is found in the crypt of the parish church at Midsomer St. Claire, which is under threat of flood from rising river levels. In this Series 16 episode, a body is found wedged under Hambleden Weir, and it bears a striking resemblance to a death portrayed in the fresco.

Hurley's village church, St. Mary's, was once part of the abbey at Hurley, founded in 1086 by the Norman landowner Geoffrey de Mandeville. The Priory was dissolved by Henry VIII in the Reformation but the long narrow nave survives in St. Mary's, with some of the monastic buildings used as a private house next door.

A short walk from the church is the medieval Monks' Barn, which was once part of the abbey and featured prominently as the cyber café in 'The Wolf Hunter of Little Worthy' (Series 22). This was an episode shot under Covid restrictions and so the production team didn't travel far – only across the road

TOP
Ye Olde Bell on Hurley High Street.

ABOVE
The Monks' Barn, home to The Hub internet café run by the maternal Mel Wallace.

ABOVE
St. Mary's Church, where villagers gather as the river rises in 'Let us Prey'.

LEFT
The daytime view from inside St. Mary's graveyard looking out onto the Monks' Barn. The Wolf struck very close to where the camera is positioned.

BELOW LEFT
Charlie Nelson, the most athletic Detective Sergeant, goes chasing over Thames weirs and bridges in 'Let Us Prey'.

for an Aunt Sally competition aced by pathologist Fleur Perkins, and 150 yards down the High Street to Ye Olde Bell Inn, where Pat Everett, played by Mark Williams, liked to prop up the bar. The glamping/camping site that Pat and his wife Ronnie liked to stay at every year was just down the road at Swiss Farm in Henley (see page 45). For this episode, Ye Olde Bell was renamed The Lamb. The abbey's former hostelry has been incorporated into the building, making it one of the oldest inns in England. It was also used in Series 20, 'The Ghost of Causton Abbey', which was fitting, considering its heritage.

"By Hurley Weir, a little higher up, I have often thought that I could stay a month without having sufficient time to drink in all the beauty of the scene. The village of Hurley, five minutes' walk from the lock, is as old a little spot as there is on the river."

Jerome K. Jerome, *Three Men in a Boat*

LITTLEWICK GREEN

BERKSHIRE

Littlewick Green can be found just off the busy Bath Road, two miles west of Maidenhead. It has a large village green – perfect for cricket – a cosy pub, and its own theatre school.

'Redroofs' was once the home of Ivor Novello, and the Welsh composer would often entertain luminaries from the West End such as long-time collaborator Noel Coward. Today the home where he composed many of his famous tunes is used as the Redroofs Theatre School – actors such as Kate Winslet have passed through its doors.

The multipurpose Littlewick Green Village Hall was built in 1911 and Novello often used it for try-outs of his new songs. It is used as the pavilion for the Littlewick Green cricket team with a handy balcony to watch the game and display the score. In 'Dead Man's Eleven' from Series 2, there is a game in progress behind the opening titles as the Barnabys go house hunting. It's not long before actor Robert Hardy stomps off to the pavilion after being run out by a schoolboy. The building has also been used as a village shop, an antique shop in 'A Talent for Life' (Series 6), and in the marvellous 'Death of the Divas' in Series 15 it hosted the inaugural Stella Harris Film Festival of Midsomer Langley. The highlight of the festival was a re-running of her 1960s schlock-horror hit *A Thirst for Blood*. John Barnaby can't wait – talk about taking your job home…

On the other side of the pitch is the aptly named pub The Cricketers, which was used as The Green Man for the Series 20 episode about endangered butterflies, 'Death of the Small Coppers'.

ABOVE
The Cricketers public house.

BELOW
Littlewick Green village hall and cricket pavilion. There is a similar arrangement in Tilford, Surrey, where architect Edwin Lutyens combined a village hall with a cricket pavilion looking out on the green.

LITTLE MISSENDEN
BUCKINGHAMSHIRE

Rumour has it that one of the early working titles for the series was *The Missenden Murders* and the village of Little Missenden played a part in the pilot episode 'The Killing at Badger's Drift'.

It is the home village of undertaker Iris Rainbird, played for all its worth by Elizabeth Spriggs, and her pigtail-wearing, Porsche-driving son Dennis, who specialise in fancy afternoon teas. Just up the road from their house is The Red Lion public house. Like many of the pubs in the series it has seen a succession of pub signs hung over its door. It played itself in 'Destroying Angel' (Series 4), turned into The White Swan for 'Who Killed Cock Robin?', The Monk's Retreat in 'Talking to the Dead', and for 'Echoes of the Dead' in Series 14 it became The Signalman. In this episode, the pub annex was used as a small hardware store run by the creepy Bernard Flack, the village of Great Worthy's peeping tom.

Little Missenden Manor is a private house which has been used many times both inside and out. In the opening sequence of 'Echoes of the Dead', Jo Starling, who works at the donkey sanctuary, cycles past St. John the Baptist Church towards the village, and as the camera pans past the village sign we get a rear view of the manor. The front can be seen in 'Small Mercies', 'Four Funerals and a Wedding' and many more, with one of the most recent appearances in 'The Sting of Death' (Series 21), where it was the grand home of shunned village newbie Cal Ingalls.

BOTTOM LEFT
The ubiquitous Little Missenden Manor.

BELOW
The oft-visited Red Lion.

BOTTOM
Only yards from this spot, Sergeant Troy was offered an iced sombrero with his tea. He declined politely.

DORNEY COURT, WINDSOR

BERKSHIRE

Dorney Court is a Grade I-listed building beloved of television companies, especially those producing detective series. While the DCI Barnabys have Dorchester to themselves, Dorney Court has also played host to Morse, Lewis, Miss Marple and Hercule Poirot.

ABOVE
Dorney Court viewed from the carriage drive, with St. James the Less Church beyond.

Located close to the River Thames near Windsor, the house has been in the Palmer family for nearly five hundred years, and though there have been Victorian updates to the exterior, the inside is virtually unchanged.

In the 17th century, Roger Palmer was a firm Royalist and helped campaign to bring Charles II back from exile after the Civil War. With the Restoration of the monarchy in 1660 he rewarded Palmer with the Earldom of Castlemaine,

then took advantage of his new Earl by seducing his wife, Barbara Villiers. Windsor is conveniently close. The countess is believed to have had several children by the king.

Charles II was the first monarch to taste pineapple, after one was brought back from Barbados. Family legend has it that he gave the spiky top to Roger Palmer, who grew it on under glass at Dorney Court. There is a 17th-century painting by Hendrick Danckerts of John Rose,

bequeathed by the owner of Bantling Hall to four villagers, with a jousting tournament on the Dorney lawn thrown in, and 'Drawing Dead' in Series 20, when it was the home of talented graphic artist Timothy Argo and his protective stepmother Dr Juno Starling, played by Jemma Redgrave.

Its first appearance was as the Fox and Goose Hotel in 'Strangler's Wood' (Series 3), owned by the socially awkward Leonard Pike. It subsequently featured as Allenby House in 'Secrets and Spies' (Series 12) and Pelfe Hall in 'Not in My Backyard' (Series 13), while in Series 21, some of the interiors for 'With Baited Breath' were shot here.

Part of the building has been set aside to host weddings, and normally the house can be visited between May and August on selected days; however, it is also possible to tour with a group by appointment.

the King's gardener, presenting Charles with a pineapple. A carved statue of a pineapple stands in the Great Hall at Dorney.

Two of the most Dorney-centric episodes have been' Bantling Boy' in Series 8, where a thoroughbred racehorse is

BELOW
Another façade of the house, which dates back to the 16th century.

BELOW RIGHT
The Great Hall at Dorney Court.

PLACES TO VISIT AND STAY

Stanlake Park Wine Estate

One of actor Neil Dudgeon's favourite episodes came from Series 17, 'A Vintage Murder', where deadly intrigue follows a wine launch at the struggling Midsomer Vinae Winery. Although there are many vineyards in the Chilterns these days, the ancient estate of Stanlake Park, and its 17th-century barn, proved the perfect backdrop. Grapes have been grown on the site just east of Reading since 1979 and now extend to over 15 acres, producing over 200 tonnes of fruit in a season. Unlike Diana and William Carnarvon's venture, the estate is an enormous success, running wine tours, tastings and hosting weddings.
www.stanlakepark.com

Bekonscot Model Village & Railway

On the outskirts of leafy Beaconsfield, the Bekonscot Model Village has been entertaining visitors, including a young Princess Elizabeth, since 1929. Roland Callingham's creation is based on the England of the 1930s, so the railway trains are vintage and the fire engine attending the perpetual fire in the thatched cottage is a museum piece. The village was at the centre of the action in 'Small Mercies' in Series 12, where Olivia Coleman plays Bernice, a woman obsessed with the place. Set in 1.5 acres, it is still a delight for children of all ages.
www.bekonscot.co.uk

The Royal Standard of England, Forty Green

One of Britain's oldest pubs, the Royal Standard of England, is tucked down a quiet lane not far from Beaconsfield. It has appeared in 'The Glitch' (Series 12) and 'Death in Chorus' (Series 9), and in 'Blood Wedding' (Series 11) Cully and her fiancé have a heart-to-heart inside the pub, while later, DS Jones has a romantic encounter outside.

Carters Steam Fair

Founded by John Carter in 1977, Carters Steam Fair is a vintage travelling funfair that makes its way around the country through the year. All the rides, including the historic support vehicles (as beautifully depicted in *Midsomer Murders*), have been lovingly restored. In Series 18 it became the Nevins' funfair in 'Harvest of Souls', and was camped out on Hollyport Green, right opposite the George on the Green pub, which became The Black Dog Inn. Entrance to the funfair is free and you can buy ride tokens online or at the fair. Details of their schedule can be found on the website.
www.carterssteamfair.co.uk